The **MATH BOOK** for **GIRLS**

and Other Beings Who Count

written by
Valerie Wyatt

illustrated by
Pat Cupples

KIDS CAN PRESS

For Ricky

Acknowledgments
Nora isn't the only fairy godmother behind this book. Many great women made it possible.
Janet Downie and the members of the Society for Canadian Women in Science and Technology helped me find
the women who were interviewed for this book. I would like to thank those who offered help and especially those
who agreed to be interviewed: Amanda Booth, Stephanie Clemons, Pat Cupples, Lorraine Duffus, Lisa Gemmiti,
Anne Gunn, Becca Hanson, Sandra Millen, D'Ann Owens, Caprial Pence, Cynthia Pollak, Nelly Simoes, Diane Sparks,
Laura Wong and Colleen Wtorek. Many of them spent hours helping me squeeze their careers into a few
paragraphs and read through many revisions, yet their commitment to showing girls
positive role models for math never wavered.

My thanks to everyone at Kids Can, especially designer Julia Naimska, who makes
writers look good, and to Pat Cupples, who brings Nora and her adventures so charmingly to life through her art.
Also thank you to Valerie Hussey, who never ceases challenging writers to do their best and providing them
with an opportunity to do so. Finally, my thanks go to two terrific editors, Lori Burwash and Jean Bullard.
Jean, math editor extraordinaire, was a neverending source of good ideas, and Lori, as always,
showed immense care as she shepherded this project from manuscript to final book.
Nora was in very good hands.

Kids Can Press acknowledges the financial support of the Ontario Arts Council, the Canada Council for the Arts
and the Government of Canada, through the BPIDP, for our publishing activity.

Published in Canada by
Kids Can Press Ltd.
29 Birch Avenue
Toronto, ON M4V 1E2

Published in the U.S. by
Kids Can Press Ltd.
4500 Witmer Estates
Niagara Falls, NY 14305-1386

Edited by Lori Burwash and Jean Bullard
Designed by Julia Naimska
Printed by Proost NV in Belgium

CM 00 0 9 8 7 6 5 4 3 2 1

CM PA 00 0 9 8 7 6 5 4 3 2 1

Canadian Cataloguing in Publication Data

Wyatt, Valerie

The math book for girls and other beings who count

ISBN 1-55074-830-0 (bound)   ISBN 1-55074-584-0 (pbk)

1. Mathematics — Miscellanea — Juvenile literature. 2. Women in mathematics — Juvenile literature.
3. Mathematical recreations — Juvenile literature. I. Cupples, Patricia. II. Title.

QA99.W92 2000   j510.8342   C00-930333-2

Kids Can Press is a Nelvana company

CONTENTS

THE MATHEMATICS OF YOU
Find out what math can tell you about yourself

Figure out how big your feet would be if you were a giant (6), whether you are proportional (8), how to measure things using your own body parts (10), whether you could fit into your doll's clothes (12), how much your hair grows in a year and other cool body facts (14).

SHAPE UP!
Get into shapes with math

Explore dimensions by folding paper shapes (18), use your bike to measure a perimeter (20), calculate area — including Nora's (22), build a 3-D dome (26) and play with patterns (28).

PARTY MATH
**Put math to work for your next party —
or whenever you want to have fun**

Make a tangram present (32), print tessellated wrapping paper (34), draw a map (36), create secret-code invitations (38), decorate with symmetry (40), play math games (42) and even order a pizza by graphing people's choices (46).

MATH TO THE RESCUE
Use math to help you out of a tight spot

Bake a cake (50), use to help you draw (52), calculate probability to win a bet (54) and discover the many sides of topology (56).

THE MATHEMATICS OF YOU

You are settling down in front of the TV when you get the creepy feeling that someone is watching you. You scan the room. There's no one there — only Fido, your cat, snoozing on the couch.

You flick on the TV, but you can't shake the feeling that you're being spied on.

In the corner, a potted plant rustles. You twist around to take a closer look. Two eyes peer out at you. More rustling, and Nora emerges.

"Are you staring at me?" you ask accusingly.

"Nope, I'm figuring you out," replies Nora. She flies across the room and lands on your foot. She peers at it, then whips out her measuring tape and starts measuring. As she finishes, Fido wakes up and Nora flies to safer ground — your shoulder.

"What have you figured out so far?"

"That you've watched 5110 hours of TV in your lifetime. That you weigh more than 700 tennis balls. And —" she drapes the measuring tape around your closed fist "— that the distance around your fist is the same as the length of your foot."

"It is?" You look at your fist, then your foot. "How do you know?"

"Mathematics. You'd be surprised what you can learn about people with some simple math."

"Like what?"

"Like whether or not your brother might pay back the money he owes you."

"Math can tell that?"

But Nora is gone, disappearing down the hallway. "Nora — wait! Will Jason pay me back?" There's no reply. The only way you're going to find out is by following her.

YOU ARE A GIANT!

You find Nora in your bedroom closet, investigating one of your sneakers.

"Nora, about Jason and the money —"

"Your shoes are enormous!" she interrupts.

"Only to you," you sniff. But you have to admit that, from Nora's point of view, you are pretty big. Your eyeballs must look as big as volleyballs. Your hair must look like thick string.

You look so big to Nora because she is so small — only about as tall as a pen. Her eyeballs are smaller than peas. Her hair is finer than thread. And her shoes wouldn't fit a mouse.

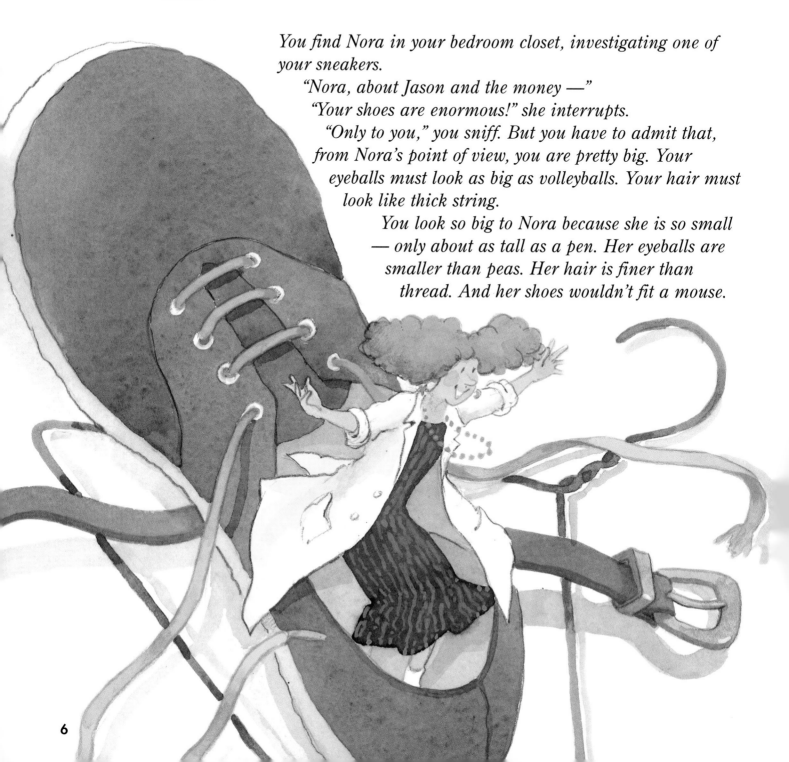

Big Foot

To Nora, your shoes are huge, but what if you really were a giant? How big would your shoes be?

You'll need:
- ▶ chalk or a felt marker
- ▶ several sheets of newspaper
- ▶ a measuring tape

1. On pavement, trace around one of your shoes with chalk. Or spread newspapers on the floor and use the felt pen to trace around your shoe.

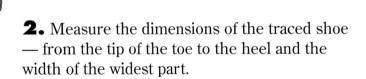

2. Measure the dimensions of the traced shoe — from the tip of the toe to the heel and the width of the widest part.

3. To find out how big your shoes would be if you were a giant, multiply the dimensions by 5.

Dimension means size, especially how long, how wide and how high.

KEEPING THINGS IN PROPORTION

Nora seems to have lost interest in you. Now she's standing in front of a mirror admiring herself.

"Perfect," she announces.

"What's perfect?"

"The way Pat Cupples draws me. She makes me perfectly proportioned."

You raise an eyebrow and get out your measuring tape. This you've got to see.

HOW AVERAGE ARE YOU?

When an artist draws a person's face, she uses a set of average proportions to make the drawing look right. For example, she makes sure that the tops of the ears line up with the eyebrows and that the bottoms of the ears line up with the bottom of the nose. The rest of the body also has a set of average proportions. How close are you to the average? Try this and see.

You'll need:
▶ a measuring tape

1. Measure the distance between your fingertips when your arms are stretched out at shoulder height. Measure your height. Are the measurements about the same?

2. Measure the distance between your elbow and shoulder and the distance between your elbow and wrist. Are the measurements about the same?

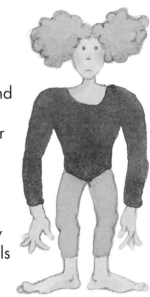

3. Measure the length of your foot and the distance between your wrist and elbow. Are the measurements about the same?

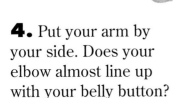

4. Put your arm by your side. Does your elbow almost line up with your belly button?

If you answered yes to all four questions, congratulations. You are one of those rare people who is perfectly proportioned. Most of us aren't so perfect.

Now try steps 1 to 3 on Nora on page 8. Is she as perfectly proportioned as she claims?

Real-life math

To Pat Cupples, Nora's illustrator, knowing body proportions isn't math — it's second nature. Pat has been an illustrator for more than twenty years. But what would happen if she woke up one day and her math skills were gone? Nora might look like this — all out of proportion.

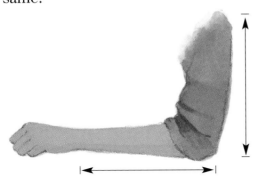

Pat knows that if the arms, feet and head are too big or too small, Nora will look weird.

The mathematics of proportion can also change a face. When Pat reduces the distance between the eyes and mouth, Nora suddenly looks younger.

"Nora isn't hard to draw," says Pat, "as long as you keep math in mind."

MEASURING YOU-NITS

Measuring Nora is no easy task. She's small and she's squirmy. By the time you're done, she looks like a mummy.

Nora unwraps herself. "I need a Normit — a measuring unit for small stuff."

"What about centimeters or inches?"

"Too big."

"Well, if you're going to get a measuring unit named after you, so am I."

START A YOU-NIT COLLECTION

Before there were measuring sticks, people used their body parts to measure distances. The distance between a person's nose and fingertips when an arm was outstretched was a yard. A yard could be divided into three feet.

Can you come up with measuring you-nits based on your body?

You'll need:

▶ a ruler

1. Find body parts with a length or width of 1 cm (½ in.), 2.5 cm (1 in.), 13 cm (5 in.) and 1 m (1 yd.). Name your you-nits.

Ha! A toenit!

2. Which of your you-nits would be best for measuring the length of Fido's footprint? Your mother? Nora's height?

3. What if you had to measure something big, like an elephant's trunk or the Eiffel Tower? Which you-nit would you use?

Real-life math

Cynthia Pollak thinks small — even smaller than Nora. Cynthia is a zoologist who studies spider webs. She knew that the silk connecting the "spokes" in an orb web was incredibly strong. But how strong?

To find out, Cynthia used the micrometer, a measuring unit that is a millionth of a meter long. (The cross on this "t" is about 750 micrometers.) Using a micrometer "ruler" smaller than your little fingernail, she measured the thickness of some silk. From that, she calculated the silk's area and found that the average cross-section was 2500 times smaller than a human hair. Then she measured the force the silk could withstand before breaking.

When Cynthia calculated the silk's strength by dividing the small force number by the much tinier area of the silk, she got a number in the billions! According to Cynthia's calculations, stretchy spider silk is as strong as steel.

ALL DOLLED UP

Nora is back at the mirror again, only this time she is wearing a black ball gown. There's something about the dress that looks familiar. Then it dawns on you. "Hey — that's my doll's."

Nora nods. "Color's okay, but it's a bit snug."

Snug isn't the word. The zipper won't close, and the seams are popping. You burst out laughing.

Nora scowls at you. "Bet you couldn't fit into this if you were her height," she says, pointing to the doll.

Why not scale down and find out?

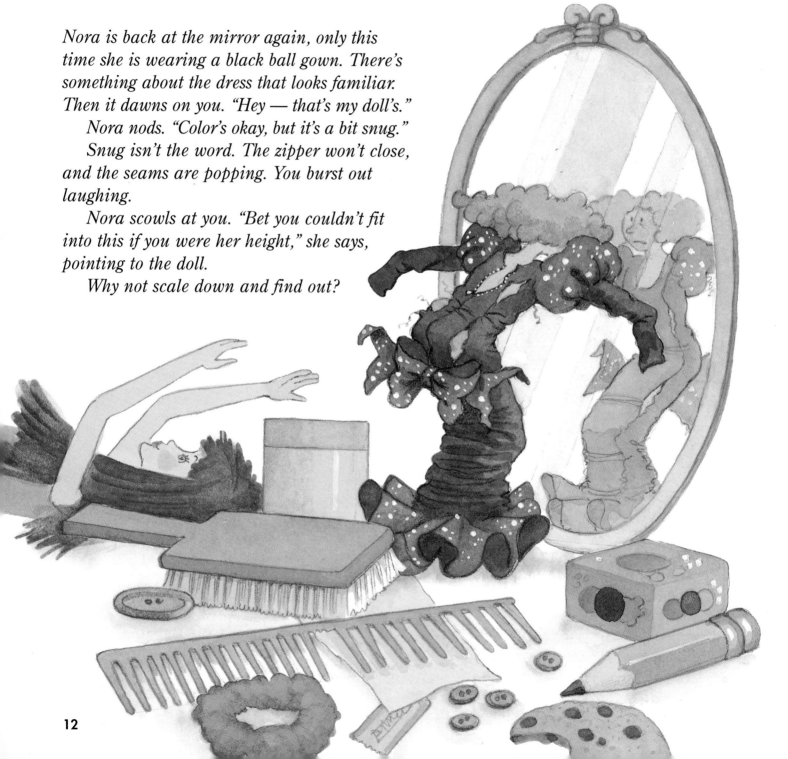

WOULD YOU FIT?

Here's how to see if you'd fit into your doll's clothes.

You'll need:
▶ a measuring tape
▶ a doll
▶ a calculator
▶ a pencil and paper

1. Measure your doll's height and your height. Divide your height by the doll's height. Round to the nearest whole number. This is the divisor.

2. Make a chart like the one below.

	Doll	Me	Doll-sized me
Chest			
Waist			
Hips			

3. Measure your doll's chest, waist and hips. Write the measurements in the "Doll" column. Measure your own chest, waist and hips. Write the measurements in the "Me" column.

4. Divide each of *your* measurements by the divisor (step 1). Write the answers under "Doll-sized me." Compare them to your doll's measurements. Would you fit into her clothes?

Real-life math

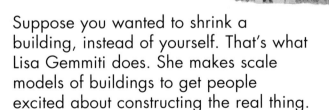

Suppose you wanted to shrink a building, instead of yourself. That's what Lisa Gemmiti does. She makes scale models of buildings to get people excited about constructing the real thing.

To make a teeny building, Lisa and her colleagues decide what size the model should be and "scale down"

the measurements on the architect's drawings, just as you scaled down your body. Then Lisa cuts out the pieces of the model, glues them together and finishes them to look like the real thing. "You've got to have the proportions right to fool the eye," Lisa explains. "Math helps us do that." See for yourself at the Scale Models Unlimited Web site: www.smu.com

BODY MATH

"Yech!" Nora wrinkles her nose.

"What?"

"You're shedding skin." She starts to jot down numbers in a notebook. "At this rate, you'll shed about 0.68 kg (1½ lb.) of skin a year. By the time you're 70, you'll have shed your current weight in skin."

"Yech!" you echo.

She scribbles more numbers, but when you try to get a glimpse, she covers them up. "If you want to figure yourself out, grab a calculator."

HOW DO YOU ADD UP?

Math can help you find out about yourself — and others.

You'll need:
▶ a pencil and paper
▶ a calculator

1. Your hair grows about 1 cm (³⁄₈ in.) a month. How long would it grow in a year? If you had never cut it, how long would it have grown so far in your life? By age 70, how long would a person's hair be if she stayed away from scissors?

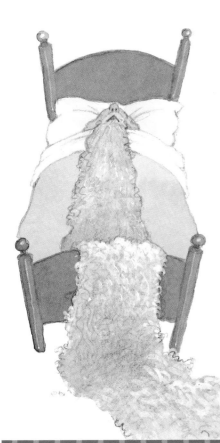

2. Your bones weigh about $\frac{1}{7}$ of your weight. How much do they weigh? What about your friends? How much do their bones weigh?

3. On average, how many hours do you sleep in a night? By age 70, how many hours will you have slept? How much have you slept so far in your life? How much have your parents slept so far?

4. When you were a baby, your head was $\frac{1}{4}$ of your overall length. What fraction of your height is your head now?

Need some help with calculations? Turn to page 63.

Real-life math

Accurate calculations about bodies, human or animal, are important for doctors and veterinarians. Amanda Booth has patients as small as a mouse and as big as a horse. In fact, her patients *are* mice and horses — she is a veterinarian. Sometimes, knowing the size and weights of her patients can make the difference between life and death.

For example, if a horse needs medication to treat an infection, Amanda must know how much it weighs so that she can give it the right amount of the drug. There aren't many scales big enough for a horse, so instead, Amanda measures the horse's girth, the distance around the horse just behind its front legs. But she doesn't use an ordinary measuring tape. Amanda's special tape tells her how much a horse is likely to weigh based on its girth. From this, she can calculate how much medicine the horse needs.

Accurate measurements mean good medicine for veterinarians. What about for doctors? Does your doctor use your measurements to keep *you* healthy?

SHAPE UP!

You must have been doing too much math homework because stuff seems to be popping off the page. A square has transformed into a cube. A triangle has become a tetrahedron. A circle is now a sphere that's rolling toward you. You rub your eyes. What's going on?!

Then you spot Nora on the corner of your math book. She is busy inflating another circle into a cylinder. What is she up to?

GETTING INTO SHAPE(S)

Nora is holding up the cube that used to be a square. "2-D or not 2-D?" she asks. "That is the question."

You answer, "The square in my math book was a 2-D shape. It had only two dimensions — length and width. But that cube is a 3-D object. It has three dimensions — length, width and depth."

"A+. Watch me turn two dimensions into three again."

You expect to see some magic, but instead there is a blur of paper folding.

FOLD IT!

Fold 2-D patterns into 3-D objects.

You'll need:
▶ a pencil
▶ 4 pieces of paper
▶ scissors
▶ sticky tape

1. Trace the two-dimensional pattern at the right onto a piece of paper. (Ignore the yellow tape.) Cut out the pattern.

2. Position pieces of tape, sticky side up, as shown. Fold the three outer triangles up to make a pyramid. Use the tape to hold it together. Count the faces. This pyramid is called a tetrahedron because it has four ("tetra") faces, or surfaces.

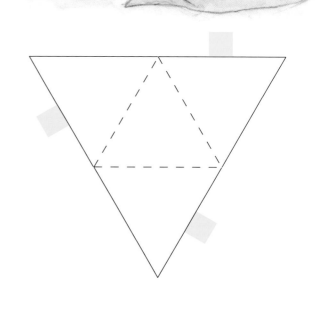

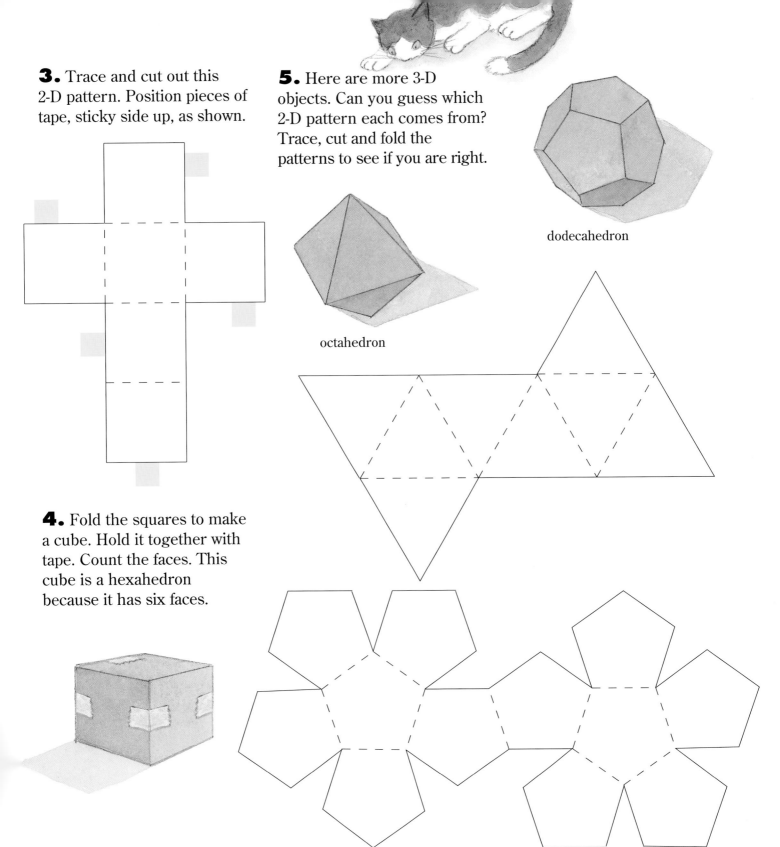

3. Trace and cut out this 2-D pattern. Position pieces of tape, sticky side up, as shown.

4. Fold the squares to make a cube. Hold it together with tape. Count the faces. This cube is a hexahedron because it has six faces.

5. Here are more 3-D objects. Can you guess which 2-D pattern each comes from? Trace, cut and fold the patterns to see if you are right.

dodecahedron

octahedron

DESPERATE MEASURES

"Get away, you mangy feline!" Fido is trying to snatch Nora from the dining room table. You shoo him away.

"I've had it with that ugly piece of fur," says Nora. "I'm going to stop him by putting a fence around this table. But first I need to measure the perimeter." She grabs a piece of tape and sticks it on her bike's front tire.

"What's with the tape?"

"You'll see."

BIKE-O-METER

Want to measure a big or odd-shaped perimeter, such as the distance around a park or backyard? Use your bike.

You'll need:

▶ a bicycle
▶ a string about 2.5 m (2 ½ yd.) long
▶ scissors
▶ a measuring tape
▶ masking tape

1. Lay your bike on its side. Measure the front wheel by draping a piece of string around it as shown. Cut the string and measure it. Write down this number.

2. Put a piece of masking tape on the rim of the front tire where you can see it as you walk with your bike.

3. Position your bike anywhere along the perimeter you want to measure. Mark your starting point with a rock. Turn the front wheel until the tape is at the top. Walk the bike around the perimeter and count how many times the tape comes back to its "top" position by the time you return to the rock where you started.

4. To calculate the distance you have gone, multiply the number you wrote down in step 1 by the number in step 3. This is the perimeter.

Real-life math

Becca Hanson doesn't have to keep pesky cats out — she has to keep big cats in. As a landscape architect who designs zoos, Becca creates habitats for tigers, lions and other wild animals.

Math is an important tool for a zoo designer. One of the ways Becca uses math is to calculate the perimeter of an animal's habitat. After she works out a small-scale plan, she visits the actual site. For big spaces, such as an elephant's habitat, Becca paces off the perimeter. She knows that her stride length is about 60 cm (2 ft.), so she walks the perimeter, counting every stride. Knowing the perimeter's size, Becca has a better idea of what its shape can be. She goes back to the plan to make changes, until the best possible space is worked out.

While Becca always liked math, "I just couldn't figure out why it was important," she recalls. "It wasn't until I started applying math to something that I had a passion for that it made sense."

The distance around something is called the perimeter.

IN THE AREA

Nora's cat problems are not over. "That's the last time that cat'll come around here," she mutters as she sprays green stuff all over the carpet in the shoebox where she sleeps.

The green stuff smells like a combination of rotten eggs and Jason's sneakers. Yuck! You've got to stop her. Maybe math can help. "Hey, Nora. Are you sure you have enough Cat Off to spray the whole carpet?"

She stops spraying (it worked!) and looks at the bottle.

Cat Off

Enough cat repellent to cover an area of 390 cm² (60 sq. in.)

CAT-ASTROPHE

To find out if there's enough spray, you must know the area of the carpet in square centimeters or square inches. You can calculate the area of any flat, rectangular or square surface by measuring its width and its length and multiplying the two numbers.

Does Nora have enough Cat Off? Answer on page 63.

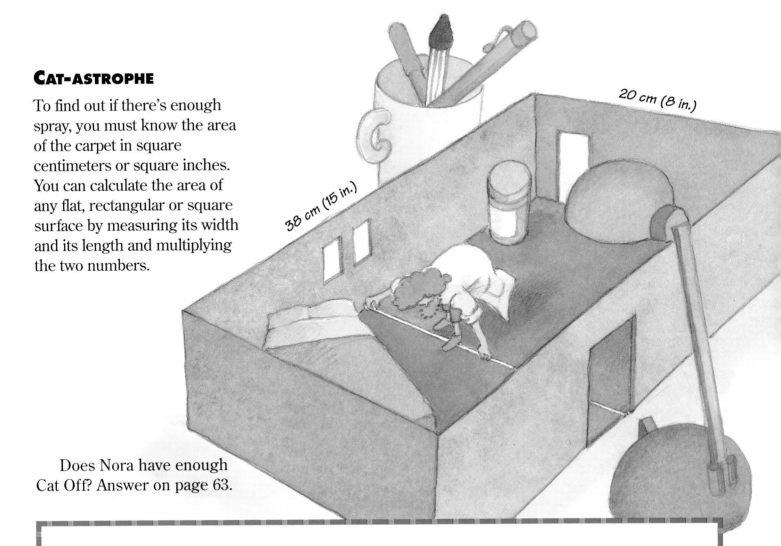

38 cm (15 in.)

20 cm (8 in.)

Real-life math

Calculating the area of a carpet is one way that math is used in Stephanie Clemons's life. She is an interior designer, and math is as important as her measuring tape. "Interior design couldn't be accomplished without math," Stephanie says.

Interior designers use math to figure out the area of homes, schools and restaurants to see where and how furniture will fit in. For example, in a school, how much room is needed for students in wheelchairs to move around easily? How many chairs and tables will fit in a McDonald's? Area calculations also help Stephanie figure out how much carpet and paint are needed and if a lamp will shed enough light to illuminate a space.

"Interior design is about creativity, but it has a very practical side," says Stephanie. Math helps turn creative ideas into real rooms that people can live and work in.

NORA, SQUARED

Nora has another bottle of Cat Off. This time, she is spraying herself. She smells revolting and looks even worse. "Spraying the carpet kept Fido away from my house. But if I spray myself —"

"You'll repel everyone," you finish. "Besides, how do you know if you have enough Cat Off to cover yourself?"

SQUARING OFF NORA

Finding out the surface area of a regular shape, such as a square or rectangle, is easy. You multiply the length and the width. But there's nothing regular about Nora, so how do you calculate her area?

You'll need:
▶ graph paper with lines that are 1 cm or $\frac{1}{4}$ in. apart
▶ a pencil and paper

1. Put the graph paper over the picture of Nora at the left. The lines form a grid over her. Trace around her.

2. How many squares are completely filled by Nora's shape? Check off squares as you count them. Write this number down.

1 cm or $\frac{1}{4}$ in.

A

B

3. Combine squares that are partly filled to make a completely filled square. For example, squares A and B (on page 24) together make one full square. Count them as one square. Combine other partly filled squares and write the number down.

4. Add the numbers from steps 2 and 3. This is the number of squares filled by Nora.

5. Find the area of one square by measuring its length and width. Multiply the two numbers.

6. Find the area of all the squares filled by Nora. To do this, multiply the number of squares (step 4) by the area of each square (step 5). Congratulations — you have calculated the area of Nora. The number won't be exact, but it will be close enough to let you figure out if Nora has enough Cat Off.

The Cat Off sprays an area 390 cm² (60 sq. in.). Does Nora have enough to cover herself? Answer on page 63.

Real-life math

When pollutants leak or are spilled, they don't form a nice neat square whose area is easy to calculate. "One patch looked like the *Starship Enterprise* after a head-on collision," says environmental engineer Laura Wong.

Part of Laura's job is to dig out contaminated soil and send it to a treatment center. After she studies the shape of a contaminated patch, she calculates how much soil must be removed.

To do this, Laura imagines squares over the contaminated soil and calculates their area, just as you used squares to figure out Nora's area. She also measures how deep the spill has gone, then calculates the total amount of contaminated soil. Laura's calculations help reduce the time (and money) it takes to remove the soil. For Laura, that's incredibly satisfying. "When the contaminated soil is gone, buildings can go up or a park can be built on the cleaned-up land."

DOME, SWEET DOME

Fido seems to have given up. No wonder. The smell of Cat Off is enough to make you gag.

You peer through the window of Nora's house. She is packing. "Are you leaving?"

She pokes her head out the window and coughs. "Have to." She coughs again, then flies over to a strange-looking dome on your dresser. "My new home," she says proudly.

Cool! You take a closer look and discover that the dome is made out of your math homework.

DOME ALONE

Nora's new home is a geodesic dome made of triangles stapled together. Grab some friends and make a full-size version with newspaper tubes.

You'll need:

▶ 65 large sheets of newspaper
▶ a broom
▶ sticky tape
▶ a measuring stick
▶ scissors
▶ a felt marker
▶ a stapler

1. To make a newspaper tube, roll a sheet of newspaper diagonally around the broom handle. Tape it closed. Wiggle the broom out.

2. Make 65 tubes in all. Cut off both ends so that you have:

• 35 long tubes measuring 71 cm (28 in.) — shown in blue
• 30 short tubes measuring 66 cm (26 in.) — shown in orange

Mark the long tubes with the marker to tell them apart from the short tubes.

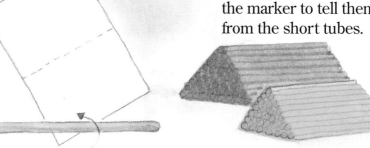

3. Arrange 10 long tubes to form the base. Overlap the tubes by about 2 cm ($^3/_4$ in.) and staple them together.

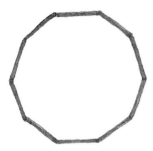

4. Make a triangle by standing 2 long tubes on 1 of the base tubes. Staple the top of the triangle together. Staple the feet to the base. The triangle should stick up in the air.

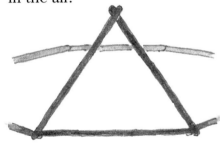

5. Move to the next base tube. Use 2 short tubes to make another standing triangle.

6. Keep alternating triangles made from long and short tubes until you have this:

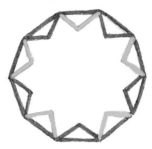

All triangles should stick up in the air.

7. Staple the triangles together using short tubes to join them.

8. Where 4 short tubes come together, staple another short tube straight up.

9. Staple a long tube on either side of each short tube to form triangles, as shown.

10. Staple the last 5 long tubes around the top.

11. Staple on the last 5 short tubes, and then staple them together where they meet in the middle.

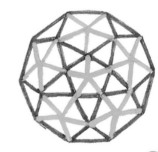

The triangle is one of the strongest shapes used in construction.

CHANGING PATTERNS

You finish your dome and decide to check out Nora's again.

It looks pretty cozy. There's a beanbag chair (made from one of your socks), a table (your jewelry box) and a bed (your lost sneaker!). Nora is arranging squares of fabric to cover the bed.

"What's up?"

"I'm making a quilt for my bed."

"For my sneaker, you mean."

She ignores you and lays out the squares in a pattern. "I just can't decide which pattern looks best."

FALLING INTO A PATTERN

Here's how to help Nora decide on a quilt pattern.

You'll need:
▶ a ruler and pencil
▶ 16 squares of white cardboard 5 cm x 5 cm (2 in. x 2 in.)
▶ a thick-tipped black felt marker
▶ other colored markers (optional)

1. Use the ruler and pencil to draw a diagonal line across each square so that it is made up of two triangles.

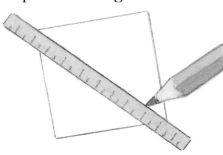

2. Color one triangle on each square black.

3. Arrange the squares as shown.

4. By turning the individual squares, can you make this pattern?

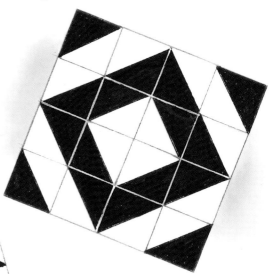

5. How many more patterns can you create by turning the squares?

6. What about tipping the squares onto their corners and adding some different-colored triangles? Can you make a bigger quilt?

Real-life math

Patterns are fun — but they can also be shortcuts, as every computer programmer knows. Colleen Wtorek is a computer programmer who writes the instructions that tell computers what to do. Each instruction, or code, is like a piece of a pattern. Once she has written and tested a piece of code, Colleen uses it in different combinations to make new instructions, just as you used the same squares to make different patterns. "Writing a computer program is a lot like putting together a puzzle, and reusing patterns of code helps get the job done quickly," says Colleen.

PARTY MATH

Your best friend Rachel's birthday is coming up, and you decide to throw a surprise party for her. What should you get her? How are you going to give the guests directions to your house? How can you lure the birthday girl over without tipping her off? What kind of pizza should you order? Too many questions. You flop on your bed.

A second later, Nora lands on your forehead. "Math," she says.

"Math what?"

"Math can solve your party problems. First things first — the gift."

THE UNJIGSAW PUZZLE

"A house, a bird, leaping horse. It's a whole bunch of gifts in one." Nora pushes some cut-up paper toward you.

"This?" You raise one eyebrow.

Nora shuffles the pieces around on the table. Every time she stops, there is a new figure.

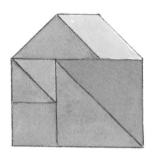

"You can make lots of stuff with a tangram puzzle," she says. *"But the trick is that you must use all seven pieces."*

Gift problem solved! Rachel will love a tangram.

CUT IT OUT!

Here's how to make a tangram for a friend — or yourself.

You'll need:

▶ a ruler and pencil
▶ a piece of paper 16 cm x 16 cm or 8 in. x 8 in.
▶ scissors
▶ paint and paintbrush (optional)

1. Use the ruler and pencil to divide the paper into 16 squares.

2. Draw diagonal lines as shown. Use the squares as guides.

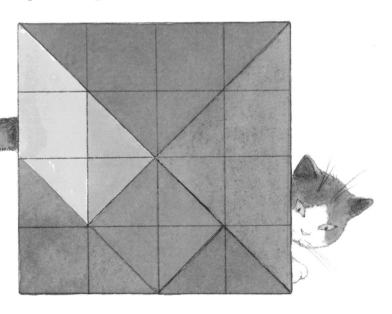

3. Cut out the seven puzzle pieces. (Each is shown in a different color above.)

4. Erase any lines on the pieces. Paint each piece a different color if you wish.

Make anything you want — as long as it uses all seven pieces.

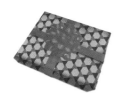

WRAP IT UP

You're ready to wrap Rachel's gift, but there's no wrapping paper. You hear some rustling and see Nora doing battle with a sheet of paper. The paper seems to be winning.

She manages to free herself. "Your wrapping paper," she says with a flourish.

"It's just a piece of white paper."

"Not for long."

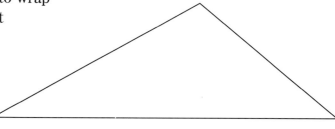

PRINTS CHARMING

Sponge printing can create terrific patterned wrapping paper. But paint can be messy, so cover your work area with newspaper.

You'll need:
▶ some tracing paper or other see-through paper
▶ a pencil
▶ scissors
▶ 2 thin kitchen sponges with small holes
▶ 2 colors of poster paint
▶ some scrap paper
▶ a piece of white paper big enough to wrap your present

1. Put the tracing paper over the triangle below and trace around it. Repeat, so that you have two traced triangles. Cut them out.

34

2. Use the tracings as guides to cut out two sponge triangles.

3. Dip one sponge triangle into paint and press it on the scrap paper. Lift it off. Make a second print beside the first. Keep going until you have a whole row. You may need more paint from time to time.

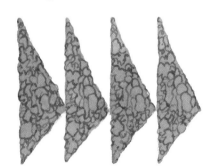

4. Dip the other sponge triangle into the second color. Press it in the spaces between the triangles.

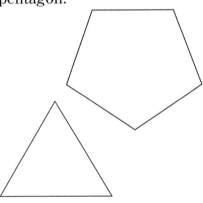

5. Now try a pattern using a triangle and a five-sided pentagon.

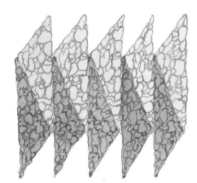

6. When you have worked out a pattern you like, get the sheet of white paper and go for it!

A pattern that completely covers a surface is called a tessellation. See what kind of tessellation you can make using three colors of paint.

Real-life math

Do you have a favorite nightgown with a wild pattern? Patterns can give clothes zing, but only if they're done right. Planning patterns is the job of fabric designer Diane Sparks. She starts at the computer and uses a design program to help her play around with the elements of the pattern, to see what looks best. Then it's time to use math to work out how to fit the pattern evenly over the fabric. "A piece of fabric may look as if the pattern is just here and there, at random, but it's actually carefully calculated to look that way," says Diane. "Math works a bit of magic."

WHERE'S THE PARTY?

Nora has been helping you make party invitations. At least help is what she calls it. Now she's covered with glitter and glue. In fact, she seems to have glued her left foot to one of the invitations.

You are tempted to put Nora into an envelope and mail her, but you need her math know-how.

You unstick her from the invitation and explain, "Some of the friends I'm inviting have never been to my house. How can I give them directions?"

"That's a snap — you need a map." She grabs a pencil and starts to draw.

MAP IT OUT

Here is the map Nora drew. It shows your neighborhood as a grid of red and black lines.

1. Sarah lives near where grid line D crosses grid line 1 — she lives at D1. Suppose she walks to the party along the orange route. With your fingers, trace Sarah's path, from D1 to C1 to C2 to C3 to B3 to B4. Is there another route that is equally short? How would you describe it using the letters along the bottom of the grid and the numbers on the side?

2. Jen lives in an apartment at A1. What is her shortest route to the party? What are the grid numbers and letters (the coordinates)?

3. Leah lives in the blue house near C5. She must pick up the birthday cake at the bakery at E3 before she goes to the party. What is the shortest route from her house to the bakery to the party? What are the coordinates?
Answers on page 63.

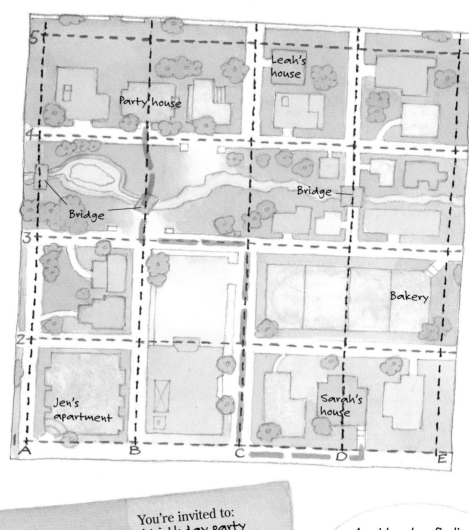

You're invited to:
A birthday party

For: Rachel

Date: November 14

Time: 2:00 P.M.

Address: B4

See you B4 2 long!

A grid makes finding your way easy. Grids can be used on neighborhoods, towns, cities, countries — even the whole globe.

IT'S A SECRET!

Everyone knows the party is a secret, and everyone is coming — except the birthday girl. How are you going to lure Rachel to your house without ruining the surprise? You remember that she loves a puzzle. Maybe that's how to do it. But what kind of puzzle?

"20-18-25 3-15-4-5-19," says Nora.

"Huh?"

"9-20-19 19-9-13-16-12-5," she replies. What on earth is she talking about?

19-5-3-18-5-20 3-15-4-5-19

Who can resist a secret code? This one's simple — once you know the secret.

1. Assign a number to each letter of the alphabet, starting at 1. For example, A = 1, B = 2, and so on.

2. To write a coded message, use numbers instead of letters. Put a dash between numbers. Leave a space between words. Can you decode what Nora says on page 38 and in the heading above?

3. You can also shift the numbers by one more, so that A = 2, B = 3, and so on. That's what was used to write the message below to Rachel. Can you decode it? Answer on page 63.

Real-life math

Secret codes are only for spies, right? Wrong. Codes are all around us — there's even one on the back cover of this book. The black bars of different widths contain information about the book, the publisher and the selling price in a code computers can read.

Someone has to come up with codes and ways to decode them. For mathematics student Nelly Simoes, getting a co-op job as a cryptanalyst (a person who breaks secret codes) for the government was the chance of a lifetime. When Nelly finishes university, she may become a cryptographer (a person who builds secret codes) for a bank, telephone company, software company or hospital. Who knows — someday you may use one of Nelly's codes.

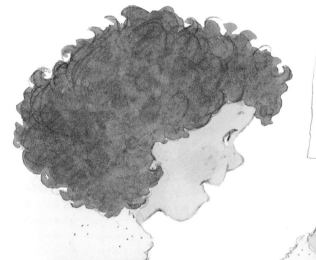

4-16-14-6 21-16 14-26 9-16-22-20-6
21-16-14-16-19-19-16-24 21-24-16

MS. SYMMETRY

Snip. Snip. Snip. *What* is *that noise? You stick your head into the living room. Nora was supposed to be cutting out party decorations. Instead, there's a blizzard of snowflakes.*

She puts down the scissors and starts to unfold a piece of paper. "Guess what this is."

"Could it be another snowflake?"

"Nope." With a flourish, she holds up a chain of paper Noras. "Notice the symmetry," she says proudly.

"What symmetry? They're just tiny versions of you."

"That's me — Ms. Symmetry."

THE TWO SIDES OF NORA

Just how symmetrical is Nora? To find out, try this.

You'll need:
▶ a pencil and paper
▶ scissors

1. Trace around the picture of Nora at the right.

2. Cut her out and fold her in half lengthwise. Is her left side a mirror image of her right side?

3. Fold Nora in half from top to bottom. Is her top half a mirror image of her bottom half? Nora has bilateral symmetry. She is symmetrical only one way.

4. Compare Nora's symmetry to a paper snowflake's. Cut out a snowflake by folding a circle of paper into halves, quarters and eighths and cutting out bits along the folds. Unfold your snowflake and flatten it. Fold it in half along any fold line. Are the halves always mirror images of each other? A paper snowflake has radial symmetry.

Real-life math

Sandra Millen is surrounded by symmetry. She is a marine biologist who studies life in the sea. Sandra believes the two kinds of symmetry meet different needs for different sea creatures. Those that don't move or that move slowly, such as sea urchins and sea anemones, have radial symmetry. For these creatures, "it's best to have sense organs all around, so they can detect predators or prey from any direction," explains Sandra. Creatures that *do* move easily through the water, such as fish, usually have bilateral symmetry. "That way, they can be aware of what is ahead of them, take in food at one end and get rid of waste at the other."

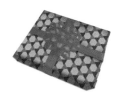

FUN AND (MATH) GAMES

The party is a big success. The birthday girl couldn't believe her eyes when her friends leaped out from behind the furniture and yelled "Surprise!"

Everyone seems to be having fun — until Nora pipes up. "Time for games."

The girls cheer.

"Math games!"

The girls boooooo.

"Sounds more like school than a birthday party," you grumble.

But Nora doesn't hear you. Or at least she pretends she doesn't.

TEAMING UP

"Before we begin," Nora calls out, "can you divide yourselves into two six-person teams whose average age is 11?"
Here are the girls at the party:
You, 11
Rachel, 12
Leah, 9
Cleo, 12
Katie, 10
Tess, 11
Sarah, 9
Elise, 13
Fatima, 10
Stephanie, 10
Maria, 13
Jen, 12

TREASURE HUNT

Nora hands you the list of "treasures" to be found.

"These sound like things you'd find in a math textbook," you moan.

"Nope. They're all in this room. Happy hunting!"

1. A pentagon
2. Some things divisible by 3
3. Something with radial symmetry
4. A grid
5. A cube
6. A sphere
7. Something with pink around its perimeter
8. A tessellation
9. Two tetrahedrons

Answers on page 63.

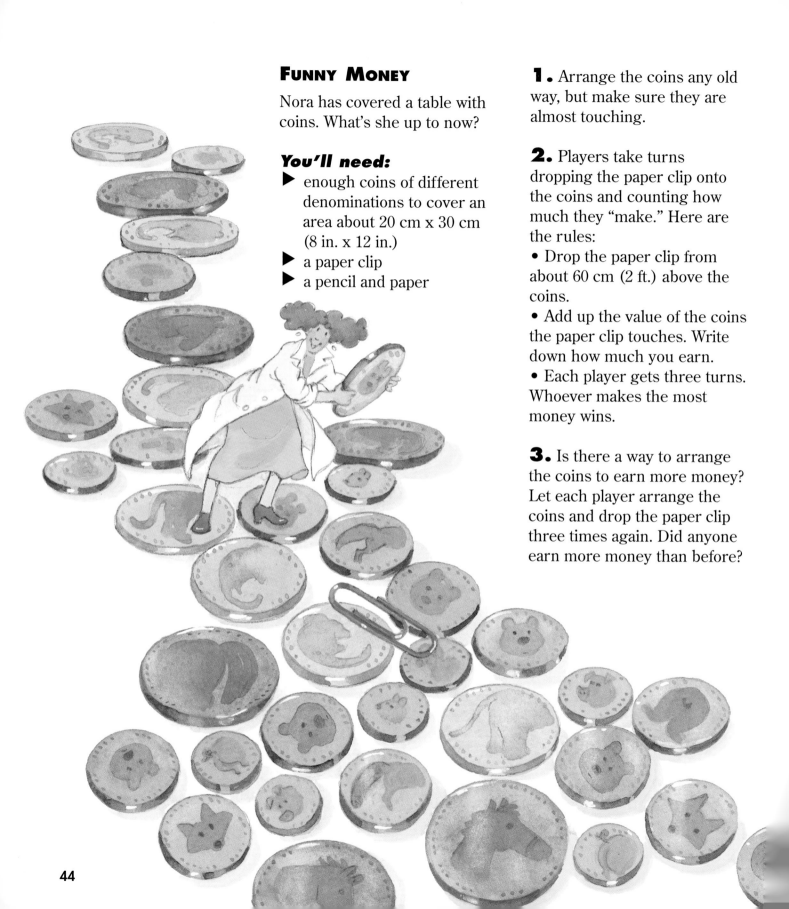

FUNNY MONEY

Nora has covered a table with coins. What's she up to now?

You'll need:
▶ enough coins of different denominations to cover an area about 20 cm x 30 cm (8 in. x 12 in.)
▶ a paper clip
▶ a pencil and paper

1. Arrange the coins any old way, but make sure they are almost touching.

2. Players take turns dropping the paper clip onto the coins and counting how much they "make." Here are the rules:
• Drop the paper clip from about 60 cm (2 ft.) above the coins.
• Add up the value of the coins the paper clip touches. Write down how much you earn.
• Each player gets three turns. Whoever makes the most money wins.

3. Is there a way to arrange the coins to earn more money? Let each player arrange the coins and drop the paper clip three times again. Did anyone earn more money than before?

Square Friends?

"Are your friends square?" asks Nora.

"No way — they're cool."

"We'll see."

You'll need:

▶ chalk or masking tape

▶ a measuring stick

1. Draw a square meter or yard on the sidewalk with the chalk. Or, inside, use masking tape on the floor.

2.. See how many friends can stand inside the square. Congratulations — you've got a square meter or yard of friends!

Pack 'Em In

Now find out how many friends you could pack into a cubic meter or cubic yard.

You'll need:

▶ 12 newspaper tubes (see step 1 on page 26)

▶ scissors

▶ a measuring stick

▶ a stapler

1. Cut the tubes to 1 m (1 yd.) long.

2. Staple four tubes together to make a square. Make another square the same way.

3. Have two people hold one square about 1 m (1 yd.) above the other. Staple the remaining tubes in place as shown.

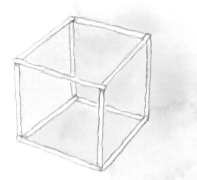

4. Your cubic meter or yard is finished. How many people can you fit into it? There are two rules:

• Don't bend the tubes or damage the paper structure.

• Only bodies *completely* inside the cube count.

45

PIZZA BY NUMBER

Nora's games have given everyone an appetite. Time to order the pizza. "What kind?" you ask. Big mistake.

"Pepperoni!" yells Rachel.

"Double cheese!" howls Fatima.

"No olives!" shouts Leah.

"Green pepper!" cries Tess.

"Double anchovies!" Nora calls out.

Hmmm. Maybe math can help. "Nora!!!"

"No problem. We'll make a bar graph and sort it out."

PIZZA GRAPH

You're going to order one jumbo pizza with two toppings. How can you decide which two to order? And how can you convince a roomful of hungry guests that the results are fair? Use a bar graph.

You'll need:
▶ a pencil and paper

1. Give each guest one vote for a topping. Let's say this is what they chose:

Tess: green peppers
Rachel: pepperoni
Leah: double cheese
Cleo: double cheese
Katie: pepperoni
Sarah: pepperoni

Elise: onions
Fatima: double cheese
Stephanie: onions
Maria: green peppers
Jen: pepperoni
You: double cheese

2. Make a bar graph. To do this, write down the toppings, then fill in one box every time a topping is chosen. For example, Tess and Maria want green peppers, so fill in two boxes in that column.

green peppers	double cheese	pepperoni	onions

3. When you are done, can you tell which are the two most popular toppings?

Hey! What about the anchovies?!

Real-life math

"A graph is a useful tool," says Lorraine Duffus. "It organizes mathematical information so that it's easy to understand." But Lorraine doesn't graph pizza toppings — she graphs money.

Lorraine is a financial adviser who helps people invest their money in the stock market. The stock market can be risky — it can rise or fall, taking your investment with it. To show clients the possible risks and rewards (gains), Lorraine plugs information about the investments into a computer program. A graph instantly pops up on the screen, letting clients compare the risks to the rewards.

"I didn't like math as a child," says Lorraine. "But as I got older, I realized that math can help people — it can even help them make money."

MATH TO THE RESCUE

Math has saved Nora from Fido and helped you throw a surprise party. Maybe it can solve a few other problems. Like your brother, Jason, for example. He keeps borrowing money from you, but he never pays you back. Is there a mathematical formula that can get your money back? You are about to ask Nora when you smell something yummy coming from the kitchen. The math can wait. So can your money.

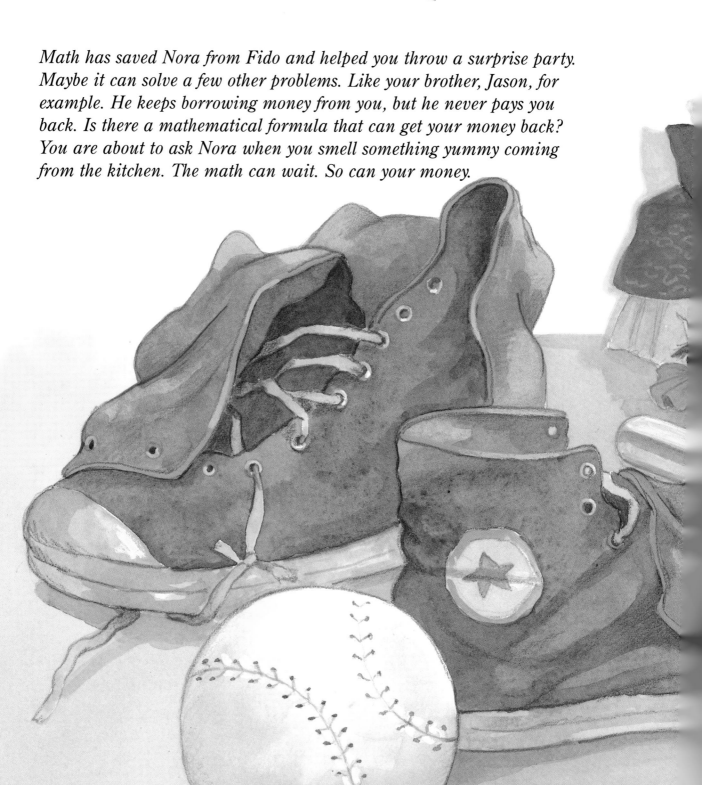

MATH THAT TAKES THE CAKE

"The math can't wait," says Nora. *"At least, not if you want to make this cake."* She holds out a tiny cake.

The icing looks a bit odd, but when you bite in, the taste is dee-lish. You pop the rest into your mouth.

"You just ate a whole cake!"

"More like a cupcake, if you ask me. Got any more?"

Nora shakes her head. "If you want more, you'll have to bake it yourself."

THE LITTLE CAKE THAT GREW

The only problem with Nora's recipe is that it makes only one tiny cake. That's fine for Nora, but hardly enough for you. You'll have to multiply her recipe.

NORA'S EXCELLENT CAKE

Metric		Imperial
25 mL	butter	1 tbsp.
50 mL	sugar	2 tbsp.
0.4	eggs	¼
1 mL	vanilla	⅛ tsp.
100 mL	sifted cake and pastry flour	4 tbsp.
2 mL	baking powder	¼ tsp.
50 mL	milk	2 tbsp.

1. Preheat the oven to 180°C (350°F).

2. If you are using metric, multiply the amounts by 5. If using imperial, multiply by 8. To double-check the final amounts, turn to page 63.

3. Cream together the butter and sugar. When smooth, add the eggs, one at a time. Stir in the vanilla.

4. Sift the dry ingredients together in another bowl.

5. Add a bit of the dry ingredients, then some of the milk to the butter and sugar mixture. Stir well. Keep adding dry ingredients and milk until everything is in one bowl. Mix well.

6. Grease a 2.5 L (9 in.) square cake pan with butter. Put a spoonful of flour into the pan and swish it around. Dump out any extra.

7. Pour the cake batter into the pan and ask an adult to put it in the oven.

8. Bake for 20 minutes. Let the cake cool before icing it with your favorite frosting.

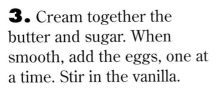

Real-life math

In the kitchen, math can be more important than a sharp knife or a wooden spoon. For Caprial Pence, a restaurant chef, TV cooking-show host and mother of two, converting large restaurant recipes to home-sized meals is just one way she uses math. In her restaurant, Caprial calculates the cost of every dish on the menu and then figures out what price customers should pay. She also must keep track of staff, food, advertising, clean-up and other costs. "It always surprises me how much math I use in my life," says Caprial. "In fact, of all the things I learned in school, math is one of the most useful."

ART + MATH = BEAUTY

The cake gave you enough energy to tackle your art homework. Your assignment is to draw a scene. There's just one problem. You can't draw. "Nora! Can math help?"

"You bet. Pick a window with a good scene."

You look out your bedroom window. "What about that one?"

Nora grabs a roll of masking tape and flies to the window.

How is this going to help you?

ALL TAPED UP

Nora is putting a grid over your window. Before trying it yourself, ask your parent if it's okay to put masking tape on the window frame.

You'll need:
▶ a small window with an interesting view
▶ a ruler
▶ narrow masking tape
▶ a pencil and paper

1. Starting at the window's bottom left corner, put a piece of masking tape on the windowsill every 12 cm (5 in.). These are your markers. Don't worry if you have a bit of window left over.

2. Do the same along the top, again measuring from the left.

3. Put a strip of masking tape between the first marker on the bottom and the first marker at the top. Continue until all markers are joined.

4. Do the same thing along both sides of the window, starting at the bottom left corner. When done, you should have a grid of masking tape over almost the entire window.

5. On the paper, draw a grid with lines 2.5 cm (1 in.) apart. You'll need the same number of squares as you have on the window.

6. Use the window grid to help you draw. For example, if there is a tree in the scene, find which window squares it appears in. Draw the parts of the tree in the corresponding squares on your paper.

Real-life math

Picture this: you're at an archaeological dig and you discover a mysterious object. What is it? A grid might just help you find out. Archaeologist D'Ann Owens sets a string grid over a site and divides the site into units — just as you did with the window scene — except these units go down into the soil as well as across the surface. Each archaeologist sifts through the soil in her unit and records

where in the grid she finds objects. "Archaeology isn't about things," explains D'Ann. "It's about the relationship between things." When a mysterious object is found, D'Ann looks at what other objects were nearby in the grid. Knowing what that object was near may help D'Ann figure out what it was used for.

WHAT'S THE PROB-ABILITY?

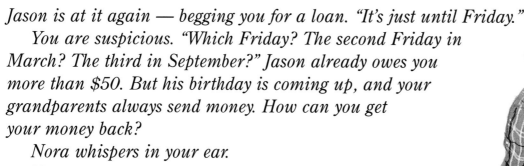

Jason is at it again — begging you for a loan. "It's just until Friday."

You are suspicious. "Which Friday? The second Friday in March? The third in September?" Jason already owes you more than $50. But his birthday is coming up, and your grandparents always send money. How can you get your money back?

Nora whispers in your ear.

You nod and turn to Jason. "Let's play odds and evens. If I win, you pay back what you owe me. If you win, I'll lend you more money — but only until Friday."

ODDS AND EVENS

Nora whispered that there is a way to increase your chances of winning a game of odds and evens. Here's how to play.

You'll need:
▶ 2 coins
▶ 2 dice
▶ a pencil and paper

1. One player chooses odds, the other evens. Each player flips a coin.

• Evens wins when two heads or two tails come up.

• Odds wins when one tail and one head come up.

If you figured out every possible result of flipping two coins, it would look like this:

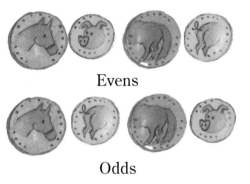

Evens

Odds

2. Flip the coins 50 times and keep track of who wins. Does odds win more than evens? Or are the chances about the same?

3. What if you used dice instead of coins? Play the same way, only this time:

• Evens wins when both dice show the same number. Here are all the possible evens:

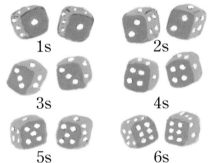

1s   2s

3s   4s

5s   6s

• Odds wins when the dice show different numbers. Here are some odds. How many more can you come up with?

1 and 2   2 and 3

3 and 4   4 and 5

4. If you wanted to increase your chances of winning, would you play with coins or dice? Would you choose odds or evens?

Real-life math

Probability is a big part of Anne Gunn's job. She is a wildlife biologist who counts caribou in the Northwest Territories. Every five years, Anne counts the female caribou in one herd by crisscrossing about a quarter of the herd's calving ground in a plane. For every 100 females, Anne knows there will be about 40 males. She uses these numbers to figure out how many caribou are in the herd. From this, she calculates the number of caribou in all herds and adds them together. So how many caribou are in the Northwest Territories? Anne estimates 1.6 million, give or take 250 000.

It's in the "give or take" that probability is important. Even though Anne's estimate is as accurate as possible, there is always the probability that number is wrong. What does it matter? Suppose the number of caribou suddenly drops. Does the decline mean people should take action to save the caribou, or is it only an error in the population calculations? "Knowing the probability of error helps us decide if action should be taken," says Anne.

TAKING SIDES

Jason has not given up his campaign to pry money from you.

You yank your piggy bank out of his hands. "You never pay me back."

"I can explain. There are two sides to everything."

"No there aren't."

"Are too."

This is ridiculous. Time for another bet. "I bet you next week's allowance that I can show you something that has only one side."

"You're on."

"Nora!" you call out. But there's no answer. You're on your own, with a little help from math.

ONE-SIDED

A piece of paper has two sides, or surfaces, right? Not when you give it a twist. Try it and see. This way of folding a strip of paper so that it has only one surface was discovered by Ferdinand Moebius, so it's called a Moebius strip.

You'll need:

▶ 2 strips of paper, each about 3 cm x 28 cm (1 ½ in. x 11 in.)
▶ sticky tape
▶ a blue pencil crayon
▶ a red pencil crayon

1. Place the strips of paper end to end and securely tape them into one long strip.

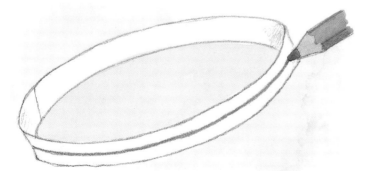

2. Bring the ends together to form a loop and lightly tape them together.

3. Use the blue pencil crayon to draw a line on the surface of the loop. Keep drawing until you reach your starting point.

4. Undo the tape connecting the loop. Is there a blue line on both surfaces?

5. Using the same strip of paper, give one end a half turn before you join the ends again. You should have a loop with a twist in it. Lightly tape the ends together. The loop is now a Moebius strip.

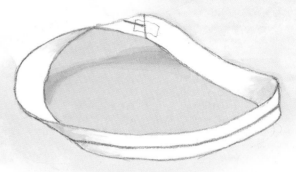

6. Use the red pencil crayon to draw a line on the surface of the Moebius strip. Keep drawing until you reach your starting point.

7. Undo the tape connecting the Moebius strip. Is there a red line on both surfaces?

A Moebius strip is an example of a kind of topology, the mathematics of bending, stretching and squeezing shapes. Now reconnect the Moebius strip and cut along the red line.

57

FIDO LEARNS MATH

"Nora! Nora!" Where is she? You could use some help with your math homework. You peer into her dome home. There's a note on the door:

On vacation. See you in $\frac{1}{4}$ of 8 weeks.

Hmmmph! Guess you're on your own.

On the bed, Fido is purring loudly and washing his face. Odd. Usually he's on his morning prowl about now, looking for Nora. Then you notice a small shoe beside him. Is it your doll's ... or is it Nora's? You look at Fido, then back at the shoe. Fido licks his chops. What's going on?

All day long, Fido hardly moves a muscle. At dinnertime, you give him a can of Pretty Kitty. Most nights he inhales it. Tonight he sniffs at it and walks away.

There's a nasty suspicion tugging at the corner of your brain. You push it away and pull out your math homework. Fido leaps up and sprawls across it. You drag it out from under him and work on this problem:

3. What is the average age of the girls on Ellie's soccer team? The players are: Emma, 12; Aynsley, 11; Julia, 10; Victoria, 12; Jenna, 14; Mouna, 12; Vida, 11; Laura, 12; Jamila, 12; Ellie, 13; Deena, 11; Maria, 14.

Fido stretches out one leg.

You calculate the average age of the soccer players.

Wait a minute. You look at Fido's paw. Must be a coincidence.

On to the next problem:

4. You are making sandwiches for eight people and want to give each person an equal share. Should you cut the sandwiches into quarters or thirds?

Fido's tail seems to be underlining "quarters."

You throw down your pencil. Uh-oh! Nora is gone. Fido hasn't been hungry all day. Fido knows math.

You grab the note from Nora's door. Is she on vacation or …

You look at Fido, who lets out a satisfied burp. It's going to take more than math to solve this mystery.

NOTE TO PARENTS, TEACHERS AND GROUP LEADERS

When I wrote *The Science Book for Girls and Other Intelligent Beings* in 1993, I never imagined I would one day write a sequel about mathematics. Not because I suffer from math anxiety. Quite the contrary. I liked math as a child and did well in it all the way through high school, though I did not take math courses in university.

It turns out that my story — good math achievement, followed by "dropping out" of math — is common among women. But without mathematics, the doors to more than 80 technical and scientific careers slam shut. As a result, in the early 1990s, women represented only about 10 percent of the scientific and engineering workforce in Canada, the United States and Great Britain. The numbers have not changed dramatically since then.

Over the years, the gap in math achievement between boys and girls has narrowed. Girls and women can do math, but it seems most of them choose not to. Why not?

There are almost as many answers as there are research studies. Some suggest that boys and girls may have different learning styles or that there is subtle discouragement of girls in the math classroom. Other studies suggest that math learning materials are not "girl-friendly" or that girls are responding to an unstated societal message that math is fundamentally for boys.

While there is little agreement about the causes, there is considerable consensus about what can be done to encourage girls in math so they don't drop out later on:
- build girls' confidence by encouraging their interest, successes and pleasure in math
- show girls that math relates to the real world — to their world — and can be a valuable tool
- introduce girls to math-related careers and the women who work in them, so that they see the possibilities and have some role models

This is what *The Math Book for Girls and Other Beings Who Count* sets out to do — and you can do the same thing in your home or classroom.

At home

- Build with your daughter. Try the newspaper dome on page 26. Building things develops spatial visualization skills (for example, the ability to mentally manipulate objects), thought to be an important component of mathematical thinking. The tangram on page 33 also exercises spatial visualization skills.
- To pass the time in the car, play number games such as "What's the next number?" In this game, you give a sequence of numbers — such as 2, 4, 8 — and your daughter supplies the next number. Play "The neverending math game" and have your daughter hone her math skills by making a long series of calculations. What's 4 x 3? Subtract 2. Then add 5. Then divide by 2, and so on.

- The kitchen is a great place to play with fractions. How long will a chicken take to cook (consult a cookbook for the cooking times per kilogram or pound). If each person eats 0.25 kg ($\frac{1}{2}$ lb.), how many people will the chicken serve?
- Going to the supermarket? Compare weights of similar products and work out the cost per kilogram, pound or ounce. Keep a running guesstimate of the total cost of all items in your shopping cart.
- Painting a room, making curtains or putting up a fence? Calculate the area of the surface to be painted, the amount of fabric needed or the perimeter of the space to be fenced.
- The garden is a mathematician's delight. Is a flower bed that is 4 m x 3 m (4 yd. x 3 yd.) bigger than one that is 2 m x 7 m (2 yd. x 7 yd.)? If 1 tomato plant yields about 7 tomatoes, how many will 12 plants yield? By spacing bean rows 45 cm (18 in.) apart, how many rows will fit into a bed 8 m (8 yd.) long?
- Be involved and optimistic about your daughter's math homework. If she gets stuck, sit down with her and work it out together. Don't let problems build; notify the teacher or get outside help if your daughter is experiencing difficulty.

In school

- Ask your students to draw a picture of a mathematician or someone who uses math on the job. How many draw women? If few, try to change perceptions by having students research math-related careers. Invite women who use math in their jobs to speak in the classroom.
- Hold a math week. Play some of the games on pages 42 to 45, or ask kids to share their own math games with the class.
- Set aside a Math Moment every day in which you pose a math problem or puzzle. Have kids start a Math Journal where they document one way they used math each day. Make math part of life.
- Let girls talk out their approaches to math problems. Verbalizing and sharing may offer some girls a more appealing math experience.
- Ensure that math classes are girl-friendly by using examples that are familiar to girls and part of "girl culture." There is nothing "unacademic" about using strings of beads to talk about patterns or number sequences. And make math classes relevant. Show how math is a useful tool in the real world, not just a problem in a book.

  If we can encourage girls to believe they can "do math" and that math is fun, we will go a long way in ensuring they have equal opportunities when they enter the workforce.

GLOSSARY

Mathematics has its own special words. As well, some familiar terms (such as "face") have different meanings in math than in everyday conversation. Here is a guide to the meanings of some of the terms used in this book.

area: the amount of surface inside an outline or the surface covering an object. For a circle, square or other two-dimensional shape, the surface inside the outline is the area. For a box or other three-dimensional object, the outside surface is the area. Area is measured in square units, such as square centimeters or square inches.

bar graph: a way to show a pattern of numbers using bars. The length of each bar indicates how many times something occurred, for example, the number of times a certain pizza topping was chosen.

code: symbols, letters, numbers or other markings that stand for something else. Some codes, such as the ones spies use, are secret. Others, such as the bar code on the back of this book, present a lot of information in a small amount of space.

coordinates: a pair of numbers and/or letters on a map, globe or graph that help locate a particular place. On page 37, the party is at B4, the point where vertical line B crosses horizontal line 4.

dimension: a measure of the size or "bigness" of an object. Something with three dimensions, such as a shoe box, has length and width and height. But a rectangle drawn on a piece of paper has only two dimensions — length and width.

divisor: the number that is doing the dividing. In $8 \div 2 = 4$, the divisor is 2. (The number being divided, 8, is the dividend. The answer, 4, is the quotient.)

face: a flat surface on a three-dimensional object. A face is always a two-dimensional shape. A cube has six faces — all are squares. A tetrahedron has four faces — all triangles.

grid: a system of evenly spaced lines that cross one another. On flat maps, the lines are usually straight. The grid we imagine over a globe is made up of curved latitude and longitude lines. This grid helps planes and ships locate places because the points where the lines cross are coordinates.

pattern: a marking, shape or design that repeats at regular intervals. A pattern can be printed on an object, such as the polka dots on a scarf, or found in nature, such as the hexagons of a honeycomb.

pentagon: a flat, two-dimensional shape with five sides

perimeter: the edge or outline around a two-dimensional shape. When you draw a triangle on a piece of paper, you are actually drawing its perimeter. Perimeter is measured in length units, such as centimeters, inches, meters or yards.

probability: the branch of mathematics that uses numbers to figure out the likelihood of something happening or not happening, such as Jason paying back the money he borrowed

proportion: a set of numbers that compare the size of one part of an object to the size of the whole object.

For example, the average adult's head is about one-seventh of the adult's total height. If a person's head were one-tenth of her height, her head would look too small and she would be out of proportion.

scale: a set of numbers that compare the size of a model of an object to the object's actual size. A doll is a small-scale model of a human. If the doll is only one-twelfth as big, the scale is 1:12 or "one-to-twelve." A model can also be bigger in scale than the real thing.

symmetry: the repetition of same-shaped parts that face each other. A butterfly has bilateral symmetry. One half is a mirror image of the other half. The two halves face each other along a central line. A paper snowflake has radial symmetry. Its six same-shaped parts are all mirror images of each other. They face each other at a central point.

tessellation: a pattern that covers a surface without overlaps or gaps between its parts, like tiles on a floor.

tetrahedron: a three-dimensional object that has four faces. All faces are triangles.

topology: the branch of mathematics that studies how an object's shape is affected by bending, stretching and squeezing. In topology, a triangle is equivalent to a circle because you can reshape a circle made of string into a triangle without breaking or tearing the string. But you would have to cut the string circle to form a straight line, so a straight line is not equivalent to a circle.

ANSWERS

Cat-astrophe, page 23:
The area of the shoebox is:
20 cm x 38 cm = 760 cm² *or* 8 in. x 15 in. = 120 sq. in.
The bottle of Cat Off covers 390 cm2 (60 sq. in.),
so there is not enough to cover the whole carpet.

Squaring off Nora, pages 24–25:
The total area of Nora is about 40 cm² or 6 sq. in.,
so there *is* enough Cat Off to cover her.

Map it out, page 37:
Here is another route for Sarah that would be as
short as the route she took: D1, C1, B1, B2, B3, B4.
The other girls have a choice of routes that are
equally short. Here is one for each. Can you find
another one? Jen: A1, A2, A3, A4, B4
Leah: C5, C4, D4, D3, E3, D3, C3, B3, B4

It's a secret!, pages 38–39:
Nora first says, "Try codes." Then, "It's simple."
The heading on page 39 says, "Secret codes."
The note to Rachel says, "Come to my house
tomorrow at two."

Teaming up, page 42:
Any combination of six girls whose total age is 66
(6 girls x 11 years old) will work. Two possible
teams are:
Team A: You, 11; Rachel, 12; Leah, 9; Sarah, 9;
    Elise, 13; Jen, 12
Team B: Cleo, 12; Katie, 10; Tess, 11; Fatima, 10;
    Stephanie, 10; Maria, 13
How many more possible teams are there?

Treasure hunt, page 43:
1. the mirror
2. 12 birthday candles
3. any snowflake decoration, the round plates
4. the paned window
5. the present with the orange ribbon
6. the present with the pink polka dots
7. the birthday cake
8. the curtain fabric
9. the pieces on the checkerboard

HELP WITH CALCULATIONS

How do you add up?, pages 14–15:
1. To figure out how long your hair would grow in
   1 year, multiply 1 cm ($^3/_8$ in.) by 12. For hair
   growth so far in your life, multiply the figure for
   1 year by the number of years you have lived
   (use quarter and half years if you want to be
   more accurate). For 70 years, multiply the figure
   for 1 year by 70.
2. To figure out how much a person's bones weigh,
   divide his or her weight by 7.
3. To figure out how much a person has slept, first
   figure out how much he or she sleeps in a year
   (multiply the average number of sleeping hours
   per night by 365, the number of days in a year).
   Multiply this figure by the number of years lived.
4. To figure out what fraction of your height your
   head is, measure your height and the length of
   your head. Then divide your body height by
   your head length. Round off to the nearest whole
   number. Let's say the rounded-off number is 5.
   So your head is $^1/_5$ of your height.

The little cake that grew, pages 50–51:
The final ingredients for the cake are as follows.
(Note: 16 tbsp. = 1 c.)

Metric		Imperial
125 mL	butter	$^1/_2$ c.
250 mL	sugar	1 c.
2	eggs	2
5 mL	vanilla	1 tsp.
500 mL	sifted cake and pastry flour	2 c.
10 mL	baking powder	2 tsp.
250 mL	milk	1 c.

INDEX